WORDS OF WISDOM

HELEN KELLER

JOLLYJOY

100 Selected Quotes
by Helen Keller

Edition copyright JollyJoy Books Pvt. Ltd.
Edition 2024

ALL RIGHTS RESERVED. No part of this publication may be reproduced, stored in a retrieval system, or transmitted, in any form or by any means, electronic, mechanical, photocopying, recording and or without permission of the publisher.

Published by

JOLLYJOY

G/F, 4771/23, Bharat Ram Road, Daryaganj, New Delhi-110002

E-mail: Contact@jollyjoybooks.com

ISBN: 9789363977471

Cover, Typesetting, and Book Design by JollyJoy
Printed & bound in India

ABOUT THE AUTHOR

Helen Keller (born June 27, 1880, Tuscumbia, Alabama, U.S. died June 1, 1968, Westport, Connecticut) was an American author and educator who was blind and deaf. Her education and training represent an extraordinary accomplishment in the education of persons with these disabilities. Helen Keller's birthplace Helen Keller's birthplace, Tuscumbia, Alabama. Helen Keller and Anne Sullivan Helen Keller (left) with her teacher, Anne Sullivan. Keller was afflicted at the age of 19 months with an illness (possibly scarlet fever) that left her blind and deaf.

100 SELECTED QUOTES

"Life is either a daring adventure or nothing at all."

*"Alone we can do so little;
together we can do so much."*

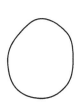

"Keep your face to the sun and you will never see the shadows."

"There are no shortcuts to any place worth going."

"The best and most beautiful things in the world cannot be seen or even touched. They must be felt with the heart."

"Character cannot be developed in ease and quiet. Only through experience of trial and suffering can the soul be strengthened, vision cleared, ambition inspired, and success achieved."

"The only thing worse than being blind is having sight but no vision."

"What we once enjoyed and deeply loved we can never lose, for all that we love deeply becomes a part of us."

"I would rather walk with a friend in the dark, than alone in the light."

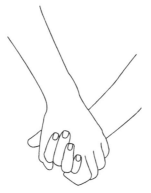

"Optimism is the faith that leads to achievement. Nothing can be done without hope and confidence."

THE HIGHEST RESULT OF EDUCATION IS TOLERANCE

*"Never bend your head. Hold it high.
Look the world straight in the eye."*

IDEAS WITHOUT ACTION ARE USELESS

*"When one door of happiness closes,
another opens; but often we look
so long at the closed door that
we do not see the one which
has been opened for us."*

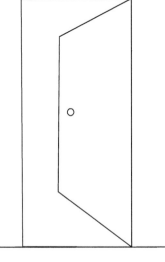

"True friends never apart maybe in distance but never in heart."

*"Hope sees the invisible,
feels the intangible,
and achieves the impossible."*

*"Security is mostly a superstition.
It does not exist in nature,
nor do the children of men
as a whole experience it.
Avoiding danger is no safer in
the long run than outright exposure.
Life is either a daring adventure,
or nothing."*

*"Life is short and unpredictable.
Eat the dessert first!"*

"We can do anything we want as long as we stick to it long enough."

"We could never learn to be brave and patient if there were only joy in the world."

"No pessimist ever discovered the secret of the stars or sailed an uncharted land, or opened a new doorway for the human spirit."

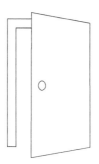

"A well-educated mind will always have more questions than answers."

"The place between your comfort zone and your dream is where life takes place."

dream

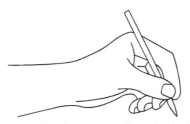

*"The struggle of life is one of our greatest blessings.
It makes us patient, sensitive, and Godlike.
It teaches us that although the world is full of suffering,
it is also full of the overcoming of it."*

*"Happiness does not come from without,
it comes from within."*

*"Your success and happiness lies in you.
Resolve to keep happy,
and your joy and you shall form an invincible
host against difficulties."*

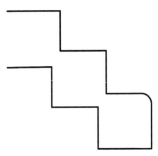

*"There is beauty in everything,
even in silence and darkness."*

*"What I am looking for is not out there,
it is in me."*

"Blindness separates us from things but deafness separates us from people."

*"I believe there are angels among us,
sent down to us from somewhere up above.
They come to you and me in our darkest hours,
to show us how to live, to teach us how to give,
to guide us with a light of love."*

"A happy life consists not in the absence, but in the mastery of hardships."

happy

"Life is a succesion of lessons which must be lived to be understood."

"Faith is the strength by which a shattered world shall emerge into the light."

*"I can not do everything,
but I can do something.
I must not fail to do the something that I can do."*

*"You will succeed if you persevere;
and you will find joy in overcoming obstacles."*

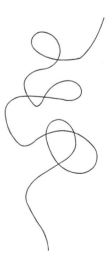

*"The best things in life are unseen,
thats why we close our eyes
when we kiss, cry, and dream."*

*"Happiness is a state of mind,
and depends very little on outward circumstances."*

"My friends have made the story of my life."

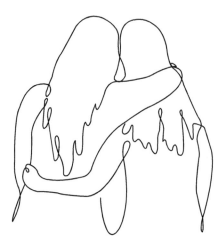

WE SHOULD RESPECT ALL PEOPLE

*"All the world is full of suffering.
It is also full of overcoming."*

*"Better to be blind and see with your heart,
than to have two good eyes and see nothing."*

*"So long as you can sweeten another's pain,
life is not in vain."*

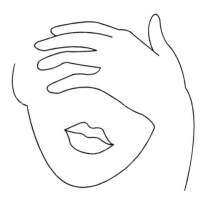

*"Security is mostly a superstition.
It does not exist in nature."*

*"Everybody talks, nobody listens.
Good listeners are as rare as white crows."*

YOUR SUCCESS AND HAPPINESS LIE IN YOU

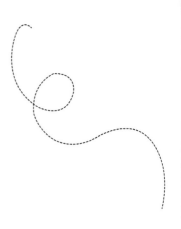

*"Everything has its wonders,
even darkness and silence,
and I learn, whatever state I may be in,
therein to be content."*

"I long to accomplish a great and noble task, but it is my chief duty to accomplish small tasks as if they were great and noble."

"A good education is a stepping-stone to wealth."

*"Oh, you think the darkness is your ally,
but you merely adopted the dark.
I was born in it. Molded by it."*

"Making a mistake is falling down, failure is not getting up again."

*"People do not like to think.
If one thinks, one must reach conclusions.
Conclusions are not always pleasant."*

"Science may have found a cure for most evils; but it has found no remedy for the worst of them all – the apathy of human beings."

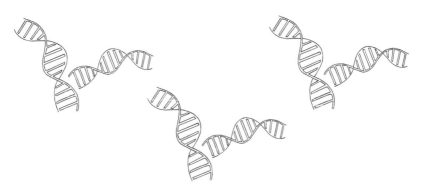

*"There is no better way to thank
God for your sight than by giving a
helping hand to someone in the dark."*

"So long as the memory of certain beloved friends lives in my heart, I shall say that life is good."

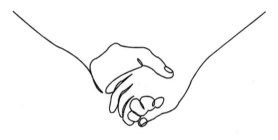

KNOWLEDGE IS LOVE AND LIGHT AND VISION

*"My friends have made the story of my life.
In a thousand ways they have turned
my limitations into beautiful privileges."*

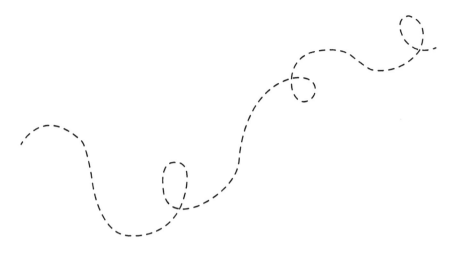

*"When you lose your vision,
you lose contact with things.
When you lose your hearing,
you lose contact with people."*

FEAR: THE BEST WAY OUT IS THROUGH

"Silver is purified in fire and so are we. It is in the most trying times that our real character is shaped and revealed."

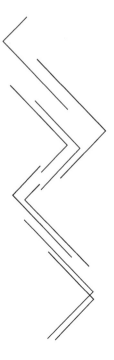

*"Believe, when you are most unhappy,
that there is something for you to do in the world.
So long as you can sweeten another's pain,
life is not in vain."*

"Smell is a potent wizard that transports you across thousands of miles and all the years you have lived."

"Doubts and mistrust are the mere panic of timid imagination, which the steadfast heart will conquer, and the large mind transcend."

"It is a terrible thing to see and have no vision."

"I believe that God is in me as the sun is in the colour and fragrance of a flower – the Light in my darkness, the Voice in my silence."

*"The highest result of education is tolerance.
Long ago men fought and died for their faith;
but it took ages to teach them the other kind of courage,
the courage to recognize the faiths of
their brethren and their rights of conscience."*

"One can never consent to creep when one feels an impulse to soar."

"To me a lush carpet of pine needles or spongy grass is more welcome than the most luxurious Persian rug."

"So much has been given to me I have not time to ponder over that which has been denied."

"What really counts in life is the quiet meeting of every difficulty with the determination to get out of it all the good there is."

"Until the great mass of the people shall be filled with the sense of responsibility for each other's welfare, social justice can never be attained."

"The marvelous richness of human experience would lose something of rewarding joy if there were no limitations to overcome. The hilltop hour would not be half so wonderful if there were no dark valleys to traverse."

LITERATURE IS MY UTOPIA

"Self-pity is our worst enemy and if we yield to it, we can never do anything wise in this world."

*"Many persons have a wrong idea
of what constitutes true happiness.
It is not attained through self-gratification
but through fidelity to a worthy purpose."*

"The most pathetic person in the world is someone who has sight, but has no vision."

*"I do not want the peace which passeth understanding,
I want the understanding which bringeth peace."*

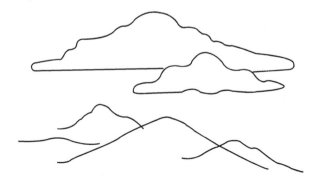

"I have made my limitations tools of learning and true joy."

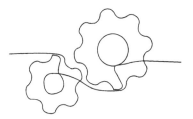

*"Happiness is like the mountain summit.
It is sometimes hidden by clouds,
but we know it is there."*

"While they were saying among themselves it cannot be done, it was done."

"True teaching cannot be learned from text-books any more than a surgeon can acquire his skill by reading about surgery."

"The unselfish effort to bring cheer to others will be the beginning of a happier life for ourselves."

"The true test of a character is to face hard conditions with the determination to make them better."

"We are never really happy until we try to brighten the lives of others."

*"Be happy, talk happiness.
Happiness calls out responsive gladness in others.
There is enough sadness in the world without yours."*

*"If I am happy in spite of my deprivations,
if my happiness is so deep that it is a faith,
so thoughtful that it becomes a philosophy of life.
If, in short, I am an optimist, my testimony to
the creed of optimism is worth hearing."*

*"Face your deficiencies and acknowledge them;
but do not let them master you.
Let them teach you patience,
sweetness, insight."*

*"Knowledge is happiness,
because to have knowledge – broad,
deep knowledge – is to know true ends from false,
and lofty things from low."*

*"I thank God for my handicaps.
For through them,
I have found myself,
my work and my God."*

I AM ONLY ONE BUT STILL I AM ONE

"To keep on trying in spite of disappointment and failure is the only way to keep young and brave. Failures become victories if they make us wise-hearted."

*"One should never count the years –
one should instead count one's interests.
I have kept young trying never to
lose my childhood sense of wonderment.
I'm glad I still have a vivid curiosity
about the world I live in."*

*"Tolerance is the first principle of community;
it is the spirit which conserves the best that all men think."*

*"A smile goes a long way,
but you must first start it on its journey."*

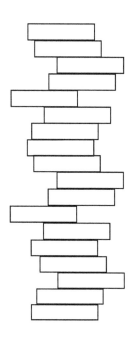

"The simplest way to be happy is to do good."

enjoy

*"What do I consider a teacher should be?
One who breathes life into knowledge so that
it takes new form in progress and civilization."*

*"Happiness cannot come from without.
It must come from within.
It is not what we see and touch or
that which others do for us which makes us happy;
it is that which we think and feel and do,
first for the other fellow and then for ourselves."*

*"If it is true that the violin is
the most perfect of musical instruments,
then Greek is the violin of human thought."*

*"Every one of us is blind and deaf until
our eyes are opened to our fellowmen,
until our ears hear the voice of humanity."*

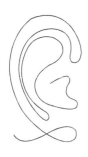

*"Remember,
no effort that we make to attain something beautiful is ever lost."*

"The way forward is simple – just follow Christ!"

There's No End

www.ingramcontent.com/pod-product-compliance
Ingram Content Group UK Ltd.
Pitfield, Milton Keynes, MK11 3LW, UK
UKHW041330230425
5589UKWH00025B/368